Stepping Out of YOUR COMFORT ZONE

40 DAY TRANSFORMATION JOURNAL

DR. VALARIE W. HARRIS

STEPPING OUT OF YOUR COMFORT ZONE:
40 DAY TRANSFORMATION JOURNEY

PUBLISHED BY:
Stepping Out with Purpose, LLC
steppingout@talktimeval.com

EDITOR
Valarie W. Harris
www.steppingoutwithpurpose.com

BOOK LAYOUT AND DESIGN
DHBonner Virtual Solution, LLC
www.dhbonner.net

ISBN: 979-8-9877190-3-9

Printed in the United States of America

To all the bold women embarking on this 40-day transformational journey, may you discover the greatness within and find the courage to step beyond your comfort zones. This dedication is a testament to the power of growth and change, reminding you that the world eagerly awaits the brilliance you hold inside. Let this journey be a beacon of inspiration, lighting your path towards a more empowered and fulfilled life.

Introduction

Embarking on a transformative journey requires a solid foundation of self-belief and affirmation. This 40-Day Transformation Affirmation Journal is designed to accompany you through your personal development odyssey. Each day has a unique affirmation focusing on transformation, paired with a reflective prompt. Make it a daily practice to recite these affirmations and spend a few minutes pondering and writing down your thoughts on each day's reflective prompt.

Transformation is a journey, not a destination. As you conclude these 40 days, remember that each day offers a fresh opportunity to learn, grow, and become a better version of yourself. Carry forward these affirmations and reflections, adapting them to the various phases of your life's journey. You are a living testament to the transformative power of purpose, potential, and positivity.

YEARLY REVIEW

JANUARY

FEBRUARY

MARCH

APRIL

MAY

JUNE

JULY

AUGUST

SEPTEMBER

OCTOBER

NOVEMBER

DECEMBER

SETTING YEARLY SMART GOALS

GOAL 1:

SPECIFIC — What do I want to accomplish and why?

MEASURABLE — How will I know when I have accomplished it?

ACHIEVABLE — How can I accomplish this goal?

RELEVANT — Is this the right time for me to be working towards this goal?

TIMEBOUND — When do I want to accomplish this goal by?

GOAL 2:

SPECIFIC.

MEASURABLE.

ACHIEVABLE.

RELEVANT.

TIMEBOUND.

GOAL 3:

SPECIFIC.

MEASURABLE.

ACHIEVABLE.

RELEVANT.

TIMEBOUND.

GOAL 4:

SPECIFIC.

MEASURABLE.

ACHIEVABLE.

RELEVANT.

TIMEBOUND.

HOW TO MASTER THE 7 PILLARS OF STEPPING OUT OF YOUR COMFORT ZONE

A Transformational Journey

YOUR ACTION STEPS

1

PRAYER

Prayer is the conversation you have with GOD. It WILL aligns your spirit and centers your focus.

2

PASSION

Passion is your inner fire, the driving force that propels you forward.

3

PURPOSE

Purpose is your 'why,' the compass that guides your life's journey. Ask yourself: "What legacy do I wish to leave behind?"

4

POTENTIAL

You are a storehouse of untapped abilities. Potential is the promise of what you can achieve when you dare to step out of your comfort zone.

5

PERSISTENCE

Persistence is the grit and resilience that sustain your journey. "Success is not final, failure is not fatal: It is the courage to continue that counts."

6

PREPARATION

By planning, strategizing, and setting the stage, you're not just hoping for success; you're setting things in motion to achieve it.

7

POSITIVE MINDSET

A positive mindset is the lens through which you see the world, and it shapes your reality. Affirm daily, "I attract positivity and repel negativity."

As we embrace these seven pillars, let's remember: Transformation isn't an event; it's a process. And that process begins now, in this very moment.

My Daily Transformation

DATE: _____

DAY 1: NEW BEGINNINGS

AFFIRMATION:

"Today marks the first day of my transformative journey, and I am ready."

REFLECTION:

What steps can you take today to initiate your transformation?

_____

_____

_____

_____

_____

Happiness is a habit.

My Daily Thoughts

My Daily Transformation

DATE: _____

DAY 2: UNLOCKING POTENTIAL

AFFIRMATION:

"I have untapped potential waiting to be discovered."

REFLECTION:

What are some talents or skills you'd like to cultivate during this transformation?

_____

_____

_____

_____

_____

_____

Gratitude turns what we have into enough.

My Daily Thoughts

My Daily Transformation

DATE: _____

DAY 3: PERSONAL STRENGTH

AFFIRMATION:

"I am stronger than any obstacle in my path."

REFLECTION:

What challenges are you currently facing and how can you overcome them?

_____

_____

_____

_____

_____

Fall seven times, stand up eight.

My Daily Thoughts

_____

_____

_____

_____

_____

_____

_____

_____

_____

_____

_____

_____

_____

_____

My Daily Transformation

DATE: _____

DAY 4: GRATITUDE

AFFIRMATION:

"I am grateful for every experience as it shapes me."

REFLECTION:

List three things you're thankful for today.

_____

_____

_____

_____

_____

_____

Self love is the source of all other loves.

My Daily Thoughts

My Daily Transformation

DATE: _____

DAY 5: POSITIVE MINDSET

AFFIRMATION:

"I choose positivity and hope over fear and doubt."

REFLECTION:

How can maintaining a positive mindset
aid your transformation?

_____

_____

_____

_____

_____

_____

Where focus goes, energy flows.

My Daily Thoughts

My Daily Transformation

DATE: _____

DAY 6: PASSION-FUELED

AFFIRMATION:

"My passions drive me to excel."

REFLECTION:

What activities or pursuits make you feel most alive?

_____

_____

_____

_____

_____

_____

Resilience is the echo of your strength.

My Daily Thoughts

My Daily Transformation

DATE: _____

DAY 7: CONSISTENCY

AFFIRMATION:

"Consistency is the key to my transformation."

REFLECTION:

How can you incorporate daily routines to ensure consistent growth?

_____

_____

_____

_____

_____

_____

The present moment is a gift, that's why it's called the present.

My Daily Thoughts

My Daily Transformation

DATE: _____

DAY 8: SELF-LOVE

AFFIRMATION:

"I love myself unconditionally and that fuels my transformation."

REFLECTION:

In what ways can you practice self-love today?

_____

_____

_____

_____

_____

_____

Don't wait. The time will never be just right.

My Daily Thoughts

My Daily Transformation

DATE: _____

DAY 9: INTENTIONAL LIVING

AFFIRMATION:

"I live each day with intention and purpose."

REFLECTION:

What does living intentionally mean to you?

_____

_____

_____

_____

_____

_____

Be yourself: everyone else is already taken.

My Daily Thoughts

My Daily Transformation

DATE: _____

DAY 10: OVERCOMING FEAR

AFFIRMATION:

"I embrace fear as a stepping stone to growth."

REFLECTION:

What fears has held you back, and how can you confront them?

_____

_____

_____

_____

_____

_____

Harmony in life is a treasure worth more than gold.

My Daily Thoughts

My Daily Transformation

DATE: _____

DAY 11: BOUNDLESS POSSIBILITIES

AFFIRMATION:

"Limitations are merely illusions; I am limitless."

REFLECTION:

What limitations can you challenge to broaden your possibilities?

_____

_____

_____

_____

_____

_____

Courage is not the absence of fear, but the triumph over it.

My Daily Thoughts

My Daily Transformation

DATE: _____

DAY 12: AUTHENTICITY

AFFIRMATION:

"My authenticity is my power."

REFLECTION:

How can staying true to yourself aid in your transformation?

_____

_____

_____

_____

_____

_____

The only true wisdom is in knowing you know nothing.

My Daily Thoughts

My Daily Transformation

DATE: _____

DAY 13: JOYFULNESS

AFFIRMATION:

"Joy is the ultimate expression of my growth."

REFLECTION:

What brings you joy and how can you incorporate it into your daily life?

_____

_____

_____

_____

_____

_____

A single act of kindness throws out roots in all directions.

My Daily Thoughts

_____

_____

_____

_____

_____

_____

_____

_____

_____

_____

_____

_____

_____

_____

_____

My Daily Transformation

DATE: _____

DAY 14: MIDPOINT REFLECTION

AFFIRMATION:

"I am proud of how far I've come and excited
for what lies ahead."

REFLECTION:

Reflect on your transformation journey so far. What have you
learned and achieved?

_____

_____

_____

_____

_____

_____

Your vision will become clear only when you look into your heart.

My Daily Thoughts

My Daily Transformation

DATE: _____

DAY 15: EMBRACING CHANGE

AFFIRMATION:

"I welcome change as a natural part of my transformative journey."

REFLECTION

How do you usually react to change, and what steps can you take to embrace it more openly as an essential element of your growth?

_____

_____

_____

_____

_____

Change is the law of life. Those who look only to the past or present are certain to miss the future.

My Daily Thoughts

My Daily Transformation

DATE: _____

DAY 16: GUIDED BY WISDOM

AFFIRMATION:

"I seek wisdom and it guides me on my path

to transformation."

REFLECTION:

What sources of wisdom — be it people, books, or experiences — are you tapping into for your transformation?

_____

_____

_____

_____

_____

_____

Your potential is endless. Go do what you were created to do.

My Daily Thoughts

DATE: _____

DAY 17: HUMILITY

AFFIRMATION:

"I embrace humility as a cornerstone for my growth."

REFLECTION:

How does practicing humility contribute to your growth and transformation?

_____

_____

_____

_____

_____

Opportunities don't happen, you create them.

My Daily Thoughts

My Daily Transformation

DATE: _____

DAY 18: LIVING IN THE PRESENT

AFFIRMATION:

"I treasure the present moment, for it's the canvas
of my transformation."

REFLECTION:

How can focusing on the present moment enhance your
transformative journey?

_____

_____

_____

_____

_____

_____

Balance is not something you find, it's something you create.

My Daily Thoughts

DATE: _____

DAY 19: CELEBRATING PROGRESS

AFFIRMATION:

"Each small step I take is a celebration of my progress."

REFLECTION:

What milestones, however small, can you celebrate today?

_____

_____

_____

_____

_____

_____

Generosity is giving more than you
can, and taking less than you need.

My Daily Thoughts

My Daily Transformation

DATE: _____

DAY 20: MINDFULNESS

AFFIRMATION:

"I practice mindfulness to deepen my awareness and speed my transformation."

REFLECTION:

How can mindfulness practices like meditation or deepbreathing enhance your awareness and facilitate transformation?

_____

_____

_____

_____

_____

Passion is the oxygen of the soul.

My Daily Thoughts

My Daily Transformation

DATE: _____

DAY 21: COURAGE

AFFIRMATION:

"Courage fuels my journey, even when the path is unknown."

REFLECTION:

What courageous steps have you taken recently, or plan to take, on your transformation journey?

_____

_____

_____

_____

_____

_____

Curiosity will conquer fear even more than bravery will.

My Daily Thoughts

My Daily Transformation

DATE: _____

DAY 22: VULNERABILITY

AFFIRMATION:
"I embrace vulnerability as an avenue for authentic growth."

REFLECTION:
How has showing vulnerability opened doors for authentic connections and personal growth?

_____

_____

_____

_____

_____

_____

The key to freedom is in your thoughts.

My Daily Thoughts

My Daily Transformation

DATE: _____

DAY 23: UNWAVERING FAITH

AFFIRMATION:
"My faith is the bedrock on which my transformation is built."

REFLECTION:
How does your faith, spiritual or otherwise, support you during moments of doubt or difficulty?

_____

_____

_____

_____

_____

_____

The strong survive, but the courageous triumph.

My Daily Thoughts

My Daily Transformation

DATE: _____

DAY 24: CREATIVITY

AFFIRMATION:

"I harness my creativity as a force for positive change in my life."

REFLECTION:

In what ways can you express your creativity as part of your transformation?

_____

_____

_____

_____

_____

_____

Patience is not the ability to wait, but the ability to keep a good attitude while waiting.

My Daily Thoughts

My Daily Transformation

DATE: _____

DAY 25: COMMITMENT

AFFIRMATION:

"I am committed to my transformation, no matter the challenges."

REFLECTION:

How do you remain committed to your goals, even when faced with setbacks?

_____

_____

_____

_____

_____

Commitment is an act, not a word.

My Daily Thoughts

DATE: _____

DAY 26: CLARITY OF VISION

AFFIRMATION:

"I possess a clear vision of who I want to become, and it guides me."

REFLECTION:

How do you maintain a clear vision of your end goals during your transformation?

_____

_____

_____

_____

_____

_____

Joy is the simplest form of gratitude.

My Daily Thoughts

My Daily Transformation

DATE: _____

DAY 27: COMPASSION

AFFIRMATION:

"Compassion for myself and others enriches my transformative journey."

REFLECTION:

How has showing compassion toward yourself and others enriched your life?

_____

_____

_____

_____

_____

_____

Excellence is doing ordinary things extraordinarily well.

My Daily Thoughts

My Daily Transformation

DATE: _____

DAY 28: TENACITY

AFFIRMATION:

"My tenacity sets me apart and propels my transformation."

REFLECTION:

In what areas of your life is your tenacity most visible, and how does it fuel your transformation?

_____

_____

_____

_____

_____

_____

Love is the bridge between you and everything.

My Daily Thoughts

My Daily Transformation

DATE: _____

DAY 29: EMOTIONAL RESILIENCE

AFFIRMATION:

"I build emotional resilience to navigate the highs and lows of transformation."

REFLECTION:

What coping strategies do you use to build emotional resilience?

_____

_____

_____

_____

_____

_____

Simplicity is the ultimate sophistication.

My Daily Thoughts

My Daily Transformation

DATE: _____

DAY 30: OWNING MY JOURNEY

AFFIRMATION:

"This is my journey, my transformation, and I own it fully."

REFLECTION:

How do you take full ownership of both your successes and lessons learned on this journey?

_____

_____

_____

_____

_____

_____

Faith is the bird that feels the light when the dawn is still dark.

My Daily Thoughts

My Daily Transformation

DATE: _____

DAY 31: CONTINUOUS LEARNING

AFFIRMATION:
"I am a lifelong learner; every experience is an opportunity for growth."

REFLECTION:
How do you incorporate continuous learning in your daily life, ensuring that each experience contributes to your transformation?

_____

_____

_____

_____

_____

Reflection is the lamp of the heart.
If it departs, the heart will have no light.

My Daily Thoughts

My Daily Transformation

DATE: _____

DAY 32: EMBRACING RESILIENCE

AFFIRMATION:

"I am a resilient force, capable of overcoming any obstacle."

REFLECTION:

How can I channel my resilience to navigate challenges and emerge even stronger?

_____

_____

_____

_____

_____

Embrace the power within you to create change; your potential is limitless, and your impact immeasurable.

My Daily Thoughts

My Daily Transformation

DATE: _____

DAY 33: NURTURING SELF-COMPASSION

AFFIRMATION:

"I deserve love and compassion; I am worthy of my own care."

REFLECTION:

In what ways can I extend more compassion to myself, especially in moments of self-doubt or difficulty?

_____

_____

_____

_____

_____

*Believe in the beauty of your dreams and
the strength you have to make them a reality.*

My Daily Thoughts

My Daily Transformation

DATE: _____

DAY 34: CULTIVATING GRATITUDE

AFFIRMATION:

"I am grateful for the abundance in my life; my heart overflows with appreciation."

REFLECTION:

How can I express gratitude to those who have played a significant role in my journey?

_____

_____

_____

_____

_____

Every step forward is a step towards achieving something bigger and better.

My Daily Thoughts

DATE: _____

DAY 35: STEPPING INTO COURAGE

AFFIRMATION:

"I am brave, and with each step, I conquer fear."

REFLECTION:

What small act of courage can I undertake today
to push the boundaries of my comfort zone?

_____

_____

_____

_____

_____

*You are a beacon of inspiration, capable of illuminating paths
for others just as you forge your own journey of success.*

My Daily Thoughts

My Daily Transformation

DATE: _____

DAY 36: EMBRACING CHANGE

AFFIRMATION:

"I welcome change; it propels me towards my greatest self."

REFLECTION:

How can I shift my perspective to see change as an opportunity rather than a challenge?

_____

_____

_____

_____

_____

Your unique journey is a testament to your resilience and dedication. Let your story be a guiding light for those striving to find their way.

My Daily Thoughts

My Daily Transformation

DATE: _____

DAY 37: FOSTERING CONNECTION

AFFIRMATION:

"I am a beacon of positive connections; my relationships thrive with love and understanding."

REFLECTION:

How can I deepen my connections with others and contribute positively to their lives?

_____

_____

_____

_____

_____

In the symphony of life, your voice is distinct and powerful - sing your song of leadership and empowerment loud and clear.

My Daily Thoughts

My Daily Transformation

DATE: _____

DAY 38: HONORING SELF-DISCOVERY

AFFIRMATION:

"I am continually evolving; every discovery is a step toward my true self."

REFLECTION:

What aspects of myself am I curious to explore further on this journey of self-discovery?

_____

_____

_____

_____

_____

The legacy of a great leader lies not just in what they achieve, but in the empowerment they bestow upon others to achieve their greatness.

My Daily Thoughts

My Daily Transformation

DATE: _____

DAY 39: AMPLIFYING JOY

AFFIRMATION:

"I radiate joy; my heart is a magnet for positivity."

REFLECTION:

How can I intentionally create more joyous moments
in my daily life?

_____

_____

_____

_____

_____

*Each challenge you overcome carves a deeper well of wisdom
and strength within you, from which others can draw.*

My Daily Thoughts

My Daily Transformation

DATE: _____

DAY 40: CELEBRATING PROGRESS

AFFIRMATION:

"I am a testament to my own progress; every step forward is a victory."

REFLECTION:
What milestones have I achieved, and how can I build on them for future success?

_____

_____

_____

_____

_____

Dare to dream, dare to excel, dare to lead - your actions today are paving the way for a brighter, more empowered tomorrow.

My Daily Thoughts

ABOUT THE AUTHOR

Dr. Valarie W. Harris, with over forty years of experience in education, has dedicated her life to empowering educators, leaders, and entrepreneurs on a global scale, always emphasizing the importance of aligning passion with purpose and building legacies for future generations.

As a minister, Valarie is passionate about guiding individuals on a closer spiritual walk with God, seeking to glorify Him in all aspects of life. Family holds a special place in her heart, and she cherishes her life with her husband, Shurman Harris, two daughters, Stacey M. Robinson and Tia M. Jones, and her five grandchildren and four great-grandchildren.

Dr. Harris's academic journey has been rich, with degrees from Norfolk State University, Virginia Tech University, and Seraphim Ministries International Bible College, complemented by her Worship Studies Degree from Liberty University and a doctoral degree from Seraphim Ministries International Bible College. Her global commitment extends to various locations, including Ghana, West Africa India, Alaska, Puerto Rico, Amsterdam, London, Brussels, Paris, and the Caribbean, with a special focus on humanitarian efforts in Grenada.

As the founder of Stepping Out with Purpose, LLC Coaching & Consulting Company, Dr. Harris's mission revolves around empowering individuals to craft businesses that go beyond financial success and resonate through generations. Her role as an author, with nine books under her belt, along with her collaborations, highlights her commitment to personal growth and empowerment. Recognition in Vision and Purpose Magazine and Faith Inspiration Magazine further affirms Dr. Harris's authority in her field, and her Real Talk Show Live on YouTube and Facebook serves as a platform for meaningful dialogues.

CONNECT WITH ME